Okefenokee Tales

By

Clint Bowman

The articles and poems in this book are mine. As the original author of them I hold the copyright to them. If you wish to use one of them, please ask me before you reproduce it. You may email me at: hausaman505@yahoo.com.

This book is dedicated to the memory of my dad, Buck E. Bowman, who taught me to love and respect the great Okefenokee Swamp.

Table of Contents

1. Introduction

2. My Father's Okefenokee Swamp

3. The Beautiful Okefenokee Swamp

4. Snakes in the House and Bears on the Porch

5. Trapped by a Bear

6. Yes, the Alligators ARE Real! pt. 1

7. Yes, the Alligators ARE Real! pt.2

8. The Okefenokee Trail pt. 1

9. The Okefenokee Trail pt. 2

10. The Movie: Swamp Water

11. The Just Seems Crazy! (To us)

12. "Post Hole Fishing" in the Okefenokee Swamp

13. Pogo, The Cartoon Character

14. Ole Pet and the Wild Dogs

15. My Little Corner

16. Eagles in the Okefenokee Swamp

17. Cowhouse Island Murder

18. Chesser Island pt. 1

19. Chesser Island pt. 2

20. Bubbles in the Okefenokee Swamp

21. Attack of the Raccoons

22. Should We Follow Every Trail?

23. A Bear, A Deer, and Some Unfortunate Bushes

24. Ole' Ridge Back

25. Conclusion

Introduction

This little book is composed of short articles I have written in the past. Most of them were originally written and posted online at Yahoo.com or at Bubblews.com .

Most of these works are of the non-fiction category. Where I relate stories told to me by others I have to add a disclaimer... if those folks were confused or flat out "bent the truth", I don't know it.

My "handle" on the Bubblews.com site was "Swampnut". I decided to leave that as a sort of pen name or nickname in this book. Also, sometimes my religious views come through in my writings. I am not trying to "preach", it is just who I am.

If you have never visited the great Okefenokee Swamp in South Georgia, I hope you will take the time to come and take a good look at it. Bring your camera, some insect repellent, a friend, and maybe a snack lunch. It's well worth spending a day (or two or three) at one of the parks allowing access to the swamp. If you don't know where to go first, I suggest a visit to Waycross, Georgia. There are good restaurants and hotels there and about eight miles out of town is the entrance to the Okefenokee Swamp Park. This is a great place to begin to become acquainted with the swamp. It is a bird watcher's paradise, to be sure! Over 300 species can be found there throughout the year.

Well, this introduction is already too long. Hope you enjoy the writings you will find within this book.

God bless,

Clint Bowman (Swampnut)

My Father's Okefenokee Swamp

by Swampnut

I remember a story my dad once told me. It was a story about a time when he was living as a boy on the edge of the great Okefenokee Swamp of South Georgia. His father was a watchtower man whose job it was to watch out over the swamp and report any wild fires which might begin from lightening strikes during thunderstorms.

One day my dad, who was maybe 10 years old or so, was walking down a trail near where he lived along the edge of the swamp. He was tired so he sat down on a large log to rest. The log was hollow and he did not realize it. Suddenly from out of the end of the log came a mother skunk with some young ones following her!

Of course, to be sprayed by a skunk is a very bad thing. My father didn't want that to happen so he jumped quickly to his feet and began to run. I asked him about what happened to the skunk. He never looked back to see, so he didn't know if it attempted to rise up on its front legs and squirt its foal spelling spray at him or not.

My dad's life during the few short years he lived along the edges of the swamp were filled, I think, with adventures. He told me of his parents awakening early and walking around in the house with heavy footsteps. They did this to vibrate the floor's wooden boards so the snakes which had crawled into the house during the night would leave.

He also told me a story of taking spoiled bread and breaking it into pieces and leaving them on the front porch at night. Then he and his brothers and sisters would hide and watch out the window for bears which might come up to the house and eat the bread from the front porch.

He loved his days on the Okefenokee Swamp as a young boy. As I was growing up, he taught me to love it and respect all of God's wonderful creation. The Bible teaches us that we are to take care of the world as good stewards. It was given to us to use for our enjoyment and for living, but we are to care for it. Unfortunately, many have forgotten that. (Genesis 1)

We who say we follow the teachings of Christ should also be mindful of how we treat God's creation which has been entrusted to us. The book of Romans, chapter 1 verses 18-20, tells us that creation gives evidence of God to those who live in the world. If we abuse creation by polluting it and otherwise killing its natural beauty, we interfere with that. Maybe it is time we followers of Christ remember one of the first things God entrusted to us and begin to recover a sense of responsibility for it. We should use it as God intended us to... with respect.

My father lived along the edges of the Okefenokee at a time when it was filled with natural beauty and he was blessed by it. Fortunately, it has been protected since the 1930's by the United States government so no one has been allowed to destroy its beauty. Today, it is a place where many go for bird watching, camping, and wildlife photography.

The Beautiful Okefenokee Swamp

By Swampnut

Located eight miles south of Waycross, Georgia, on U.S highway 1 is a junction where adventurous travelers, bird watchers, and nature enthusiasts can enter the still wild Okefenokee Swamp. Located at the terminus of a causeway traversing Cowhouse Island and its surrounding watery prairies, sits a small park called the Okefenokee Swamp Park. The park was created in the 1940's, and its mission statement states that the park's mission is to promote ecological tourism and to educate visitors about the incredible swamp and its very diverse population of animal and plant life. The park's website gives a good introduction to the park, its history, and purpose. The nearby town of Waycross has plenty of nice hotels and restaurants to make such an experience very pleasurable and affordable as well.

As one who grew up on this northern edge of the swamp, a son whose father was partially raised along its edges as well, I can promise any adventurer that the Okefenokee Swamp is well worth a prolonged visit. I have been camping within the swamp several times. On one occasion I led a group of teenaged young men and their chaperones from the Kingfisher landing located between Waycross and Folkston, Georgia, down through the swamp to the southern edge where we exited at the beautiful and remote Stephen C. Foster state park entrance. This is one of the few locations where fishermen and canoeing/kayaking nature lovers can enter and exit the National Wildlife Refuge which covers the great majority of the swamp.

 Of course, anyone heading through the swamp on such an excursion may hope to see any number of birds of all sizes, a few snakes here and there and the almost always viewable American alligator. There are over 250 species of birds found within the swamp and its bordering regions. The swamp and its surrounding terrain is also the home of panthers, bobcats, bears, whitetail deer, wild turkeys, river otters, and numerous other critters. Bring your camera and keep it ready at hand as you travel through the swamp. Opportunities to capture photographic evidence to back up your claims of seeing "this and that" will occur suddenly and then be quickly gone. The wildlife of the Okefenokee is secretive and very shy around humans. Especially the deer, bears, bobcats, and panthers.

I love visiting the swamp even if only for a few hours or one day.

Hope to see you there soon!

Snakes in the House and Bears on the Porch

By Swampnut

As I have stated in other writings, my dad spent his childhood on the Okefenokee Swamp. For a period of time they lived at Black Hammock which is kind of up on the northwest side of the current wildlife refuge boundaries. At another time they lived at the settlement known as Braganza which straddled the old stagecoach line and rail line along the north side of the swamp. The settlement is near the well known Cowhouse Island.

He once told me that at times in warmer weather, his parents would get up early in the morning, shout for the children to stay on their beds, and then walk around stomping the floor. This was so the snakes which may have entered the house through the cracks in the floors would feel the vibrations and hide or leave.

One of my aunts told me that one time she was helping her mom in the kitchen doing some baking. She reached up on a shelf to get some flour... and discovered that a rat snake had chosen that as his hiding place! I think grandmother got the snake and threw it out of the house.

Another time both my dad and the same sister told of leaving stale bread on the front porch and hiding to watch the black bears come up on the porch and eat it at night. I am not sure I would have wanted to do that. Especially since the windows had no screens and were open.

They did have curtains and shutters which could be closed as needed.

Trapped by a Bear

By Swampnut

This is a story told to me by one of my aunts, a sister of my dad. She is the last remaining one of that generation of my family still living in South Georgia. A couple of years ago, she told me about a time when she had been up in the fire watchtower which my grandfather was paid to man out on the Okefenokee Swamp. He trained 2-3 of his children to know how to use the sighting equipment up in the tower so they could sometimes sit up there and look for smoke out over the swamp. They enjoyed doing it. She told me she really enjoyed the view and the solitude up there. If they saw smoke they would shout down for my grandfather. He would then stop whatever work he was doing and climb up to confirm it and call it in to his headquarters. She was about eleven years old, maybe twelve at the time.

Grandfather was down on the ground, probably doing some repair or other at the little house they lived in. My aunt opened the trapdoor in the floor to begin to climb down the steps. She was very surprised to see a black bear climbing UP the tower's steps! She immediately closed the door and bolted it, I believe. She then began to call out for help. My dad heard her first and came running to see what was happening, then grandfather came. He sent my dad to the house to bring the old shotgun.

Then, if I remember the story correctly, he fired it in the air to frighten the bear. He had already called up to my aunt that she should remain calm and "Everything would be okay." Also, that she should keep the trapdoor closed...which probably was an unnecessary thing to say, I'm sure.

After a couple of shotgun blasts, I believe the bear decided he needed to leave. He scampered down and took off into the nearby brush. Then my aunt could come down for supper... which is, I believe, the reason she had started down the first time.

"Yes, the alligators ARE real!" (pt 1)

by Swampnut

At the tender young age of eighteen, I had the privilege of working as a swamp tour guide at the Okefenokee Swamp Park located in South Georgia. I had finished high school early that spring. This was partly due to the fact that I had enough units to graduate. It was also due to the advice of the school counselor who basically told me I needed to get out before I got in too much trouble and missed graduation. I was not a problem student, but I did tend to live daily "close to the line" which frustrated many of those who were much more serious about the field of education... such as my teachers.

I had already enlisted on a delayed entry program for the US Army, so it just made sense to them to suggest that I leave school and "enjoy life" before I went off to the army that summer. My parents were surprised, and at first assumed I had been expelled for some yet-to-be-learned reason. I crashed on the couch for about 6-7 days and that didn't sit well with two hard working parents, so they rather seriously encouraged me to get a job. Hence, the job in the Okefenokee swamp as a guide.

One of the most frustrating things we dealt with there were the tourists who came through from up north (where I was surprised to learn they don't have alligators). These folks often didn't believe us as we shared with them the info on the swamp and its assortment of critters. (If you go to www.okeswamp.com you can find info on the swamp and its critters.) The most famous type of animal most tourists were eager to see were the alligators. There was one which lived in the park and hung out near the main park area. He had been named Oscar many years ago by one of the park's employees. He liked to rest out in the sun on a small island of grass in a little pond-like area near the interpretive center.

During a time when the water level had dropped quite low in the swamp, the water around the little island of grass had almost totally dried up. One morning, one of our guides came walking along the nearby sidewalk and discovered that a lady had walked out to Oscar and was sitting on this huge alligator as he slept! Her husband was busy snapping her picture and the guide almost fainted! Oscar was about 15 feet long and when he slept on land, he looked fake. This woman thought he was fake and at first didn't really trust the guide, who had erupted into a frenzy of excitement and was loudly pleading with her to get off Oscar and get back over to the sidewalk.

After a moment or two, the lady realized that the guide was indeed serious and she walked back over to where her husband was. Turning around and looking back at Oscar, she then, almost fainted... as Oscar slowly lumbered down off the grassy mound and into the little bit of water still remaining behind the island! Only the Good Lord above saved that woman that day.

Oscar died much later. His skeleton is preserved in the gift shop there at the swamp in a glass case for visitors to view.

"Yes, the alligators ARE real!" (pt2)

by Swampnut

On another occasion, I had a group out on the short boat tour. This was about a 25 minute boat tour which looped around through some of the more interesting areas nearby. The trail went through a forested area, then an area of thick "hurrah" bushes and then around into a semi-prairie area before reentering the more forested areas and returning to the boat dock.

We would ride through Mirror Lake, so named because a sign nailed to a nearby tree could clearly be seen reflecting in the dark looking swamp waters. We would also ride through a place called Skull Lake which had a few cattle skulls nailed or lodged in trees. The rumor was that in olden days it was thought that Native Americans had made some sort of animal sacrifices there because early settlers found several cattle skulls in the lake.

This particular morning, we were riding slowly along and I was pointing out a small alligator of only about 4 feet in length which was sunning on a large clump of grasses. Just moments before I had pointed out a harmless snake of about 2 feet in length which was sunning on a limb we had floated under. As I was talking, a lady turned and asked very seriously, "Isn't it true that earlier this morning you people came out and set these animals up for us to see?"

I was flabbergasted! These were completely wild animals! The park is actually a very small part of what is a huge National Wildlife Refuge covering hundreds of square miles. The idea that we would do such a thing completely startled me. And on top of that, how in the world would we have convinced the animals to stay put if we did "set them up" to be seen??

I am afraid that I was so startled by the ridiculousness of the question, that my simple "No!" didn't sound very convincing to her. Believe me folks; the alligators (and all the other animals) ARE REAL AND WILD.

The Okefenokee Trail (pt 1)

by Swampnut

This may sound like a trail which an adventurous traveler might follow through remote and dangerous places. Or a type of trail which might lead to some long forgotten ghostly place once settled by an ancient people. Or maybe even a trail which might lead through some ancient land to a place of romance and adventure. BUT…. it is not any of these, at least not exactly.

The Okefenokee Trail was created by an act of the Georgia State Legislature, not an ancient tribal group or band of explorers. The act is called House Resolution 1661 and dedicates the Okefenokee Trail and the renaming of a bridge near the town of Folkston, Georgia, in honor of a man by the name of Herschel Stokes. It is a system of paved roads which largely encircle the great Okefenokee Swamp of South Georgia.

This system of roads includes state route 177.

This road enters the north side of the Okefenokee Swamp and exits the south side... but the two ends do not connect! There is NO road going through the heart of the swamp! So....what lies between the two ends of the interrupted state route 177? That's a topic for a different post! (Stay tuned)

The Okefenokee Trail (pt 2)

by Swampnut

So...what lies between the ends of interrupted state route 177 in the heart of the great Okefenokee Swamp? Good question! One fellow long ago apparently thought there was a cave in there. To have a cave, I think you would at least need to have a hill or mountain...no such thing in the Okefenokee. The fellow was a song writer who wrote a song titled "Miller's Cave". It became a hit of sorts in the early 1960's. The song was recorded by Bobbie Bare, Hank Snow, Charley Pride, and other country singers. You can listen to it on any of several internet sites. So...there is no cave.
So, what is there to be seen? Well, if you use a map to plot your route traveling south down highway 177, you come to a dead end

in the swamp at a place called Okefenokee Swamp Park. This is a privately owned and run park created to educate folks about the swamp. But those of us, who know better, know that a person could take a boat and make his way southwards through several beautiful lakes and trails to the south side of the swamp and meet up with state highway 177 again.

Along the way, one would pass through such places as Green River (not really a river), Mud Lake (not really muddy), Maul Hammock Lake, Dinner Pond, Big Water (A movie once filmed in the swamp had this name as its title), Minnie's Lake, and finally Billy's Lake (possibly named after Chief Billy Bowlegs, the last Seminole war chief to live in the swamp). Along the way one would spot numerous birds of all sizes and colors. Alligators and turtles would be scattered all around you. Fish might leap out of the lily pad covered waters to escape your boat...they sometimes mistakenly will even land in the boat! The really fortunate traveler might get a glimpse of a bobcat or even a panther or black bear. The swamp is a great place to visit, especially for bird watching and wildlife photography. Camping and fishing are usually fun activities there as well.

So, now you know the whole story of the Okefenokee Trail. Come on, pack up and come for a visit!

Those wanting a more colorful (literally) explanation of this route can find it at www.OkefenokeeTrail.org

The Movie: Swamp Water

by Clint Bowman

Many of you older folks will know who Walter Brennan was. Brennan lived from 1894 to 1974 and was a World War 1 veteran. A role I remember him fondly in was the one of deputy Stumpy in John Wayne's movie "Rio Bravo". Brennan was a man of Christian faith and would sometimes be seen at Billy Graham crusades where he would speak briefly. He was the lead actor in the movie Swamp Water. This movie was made in 1941 in the Okefenokee Swamp near Waycross.

In the movie, Brennan is hiding in the swamp after being falsely accused of murder. He makes friends with a young boy who lives on the edge of the swamp and that young boy helps out by selling animal skins which Walter Brennan brings to him. Of course, the townsfolk eventually figure it out and then the trouble begins!

The movie also starred Dana Andrews, Walter Huston, and Anne Baxter. It cost about $600,000 to make, which I guess was a sizable amount of money in those days. The movie turned a profit and was somewhat popular. It was produced by Twenty Century Fox and was based on a novel written by Georgia writer Vereen Bell.

In 1952 the movie was remade as "Lure of the Wilderness".
It is easily viewable online, I believe.

That Just Seems Crazy! (To us)

By Swampnut

Recently, I heard of a group of businessmen who come to south Georgia once a year for a week of fishing in the Okefenokee Swamp. Now fishing in the swamp is NOT a crazy thing to do. In fact, it is very rewarding.
But these fellows fish for "mud fish"! The proper name is bowfin. Most of us who grew up down here, REALLY don't like these fish. They are thick as gnats in the swamp. They don't taste good unless you have some secret way of cooking them and if it isn't done correctly, the meat turns almost to mush when cooked. (I know of NO ONE who cooks them).
However, these fish fight like demons when caught. They have a long fin down their back and another underneath and when you hook one, he will turn sideways and it feels as if you are pulling up a tree!
No one I know can understand why anyone

would pay out so much money to fish for "mudfish". Even if you are fishing for blue gill or other types of fish, you have a good chance of one of these predators grabbing your bait, so why go out of your way for such a difficult and nasty fish??

Maybe these fellows from up north have some secret recipe for cooking these things. Who knows?

"Post Hole Fishing" in the Okefenokee Swamp

By Swampnut

Well, if you were attracted to this article by seeing the title, I bet you are wondering what the heck this is about.

Recently, a couple of folks entertained some of us who are members of a particular Facebook group with some comments about fishing in post holes in the Okefenokee Swamp. Now the swamp, according to testimony of all of those who have been in it, is filled with a watery ecosystem so digging post holes in it for fishing purposes doesn't make a lot of sense.

However, this particular swamp has a secret. Okefenokee is an old Indian word which loosely translates "land of the trembling earth". In fact that is the accepted nickname for the Okefenokee Swamp.

The swamp isn't stagnant (in fact, two rivers flow out of it). It is actually an ancient lake which was formed in ancient times when the ocean levels dropped and the shoreline receded to its present boundaries along the Georgia coast. A barrier ridge of sand held the water in a large depression and formed the lake. Gradually over time plants of various types grew and died along its edges. The dead matter sank into the waters and covered the bottom of the lake.

As the dead plant matter degrades, it forms methane gas. When enough pressure builds, the gas seeks to escape and bubbles its way to the surface. It often pushes to the surface some of that decaying plant material. This floats and grass and plant seeds are deposited on it by winds or wildlife. Eventually many will germinate and grow. As the various grasses and plants grow, their roots intertwine and as a result it strengthens the floating "island" of grass and plants. Some of these islands are so large that a traveler canoeing through the area may think he has found one of the swamp's islands.

However, if you disembark your boat or canoe and stand on one of these "islands" you will soon discover that it is actually floating on water. If you bounce a bit, you may even see nearby bushes and small trees bobbing slightly as the ripple effect of your bouncing hits their location.

Beneath these floating islands of course, the water may be anywhere from 1-10 feet deep. It is through these "islands" that a few old time swampers used to use post hole diggers to dig "post holes" through the mass. And they would then fish in these holes. Of course, their baited line would dangle down into an open water area filled with fish, turtles, and the frequently sighted alligators the swamp is well known for.

Hence...the title "Post Hole Fishing" in the Okefenokee Swamp.

Pogo, the Cartoon Character

By Swampnut

An American cartoonist by the name of Walt Kelly created the Pogo cartoon script. It was set in the Okefenokee Swamp and featured a loveable opossum by the name of Pogo. He had a cast of other critters who helped him philosophize about life.

Some of Pogo's friends were Albert the Alligator, Howland Owl, a mud turtle known as Churchill "Churchy" La Femme, some variation of a hound dog named Beauregard Bugleboy and many, many others.

The cartoon script ran from about 1948 to 1975. It is hilarious fun to read even today, if you can find it.

You can find far more than you might really want to know about it by searching Wikipedia for "Pogo (the comic script)".

Added note: After publishing this article, I visited the Okefenokee Swamp Park near Waycross. As we toured the park, we attended a wildlife show held in the theater of the snake house or what they call the "serpentarium". After you exit the theater, you enter a small foyer where a very informative exhibit about Walt Kelly and his cartoon work is viewable. It is worth taking the time to browse through it. You will enjoy it.

Ole' Pet and the Wild Dogs

By Swampnut

As I have stated in other pieces I have written, my dad spent his childhood out on the edge of the Okefenokee Swamp. It appears to have been a perfect place for a young boy to learn and grow. However, my dad's parents died within 6 months of each other when he was about 13. Dad had to then move to town and live with an aunt who was widowed, had at least 2 children of her own... one a special needs child. It was a very poor and hard way to grow into adulthood in the 1940's.

One of the stories my dad told me from his earlier years on the swamp involved the family mule named Ole' Pet. My grandfather was a watchtower man who worked for the forestry department. For a time they lived at Black Hammock out on the northwest side of the swamp. One day he had given my dad the task of plowing corn with the mule while he was up looking out over the swamp for a fire. Lightening starts frequent fires out there so he was often kept busy checking for them and reporting them.

As my dad began plowing the old mule did well. But after a bit she began to act up each time he approached the far end of the field. She would obey, but grudgingly. After 2-3 times of this my grandfather came down the tower ladder calling for my dad to stop immediately.

Turns out, he had glanced around to check on how dad was doing... and spotted a pack of wild dogs creeping up through the woods to ambush Ole' Pet and dad. Dad returned to the tower with the mule and my grandfather sent him up to the house to bring his double barreled shotgun. I am not sure what became of the dogs, but that was the day my grandfather taught my dad how to fire the shotgun. My dad was too small to shoulder it well, so grandpa taught him how to back up against a tree and brace himself so he could fire it.

After that day, any time dad plowed, he carried the gun to the field and kept it leaning against a tree or stump nearby.

My Little Corner

by Swampnut

Slowly the paddle dipped into the still dark waters,
Nearby a bullfrog croaks greetings.
A red winged blackbird sweeps across...
Landing on a cattail, he sings out his welcome.

The gently dancing white water lily flowers...
Their yellow centers brightly bobbing here and there,
Give birth suddenly to a leaping bright green grasshopper.
His refuge no longer the safe haven he thought ...
Watery ripples pass over his yellow throne.

The cool and gentle evening breeze,
Passing through at the end of hot day,
Welcomes me back to my little island.
My hidden, blessed little corner of the world.

Eagles in the Okefenokee Swamp

By Swampnut

That title might be a little misleading, but I don't think so. Today, my wife and I drove south from Georgia down to Tampa for a meeting. Since we live on the north side of this great Swamp, we had to go around it to head south. Our Garmin GPS wanted us to go west to hit I-75, but we felt that it was taking us too far west before turning south.

We decided to travel slightly west of town and then take a smaller paved road which runs along the western edge of the swamp down to highway 141 and then follow it the rest of the way around to the southwest corner of the swamp and then southwards down into Florida. Anyone who knows those roads knows how remote that area is. It was down there somewhere along highway 141 skirting the corner of the swamp that we saw the first Bald eagle we have seen in the swamp... ever!

But... he was not being majestic and acting heroic.... he was eating a dead raccoon along the side of the road. One which a vehicle had killed, probably during the night. I'm afraid we disturbed his lunch while we took his picture. He flew up into a large pine tree and waited for us to leave.

Cowhouse Island Murder

(The death of Jack Hagin)

I've heard rumors of late,

Of a man, met with ill-fate.

Hauling supplies,

A load of crossties.

A shot rang out,

No one about!

Who felled this man, this son and brother?

Unknown, the secret lies with another.

By Clint Bowman

Nov. 2014

I was inspired to write this poem a few weeks after reading about the murder of Jack Hagin in the book "The Forgotten Families of

Cowhouse Island". The book was written by Manda Lee Johns.

Chesser Island (Pt 1)

by Swampnut

Usually one thinks of alligators attacking the unwary when topics such as swamps are brought up in discussion. However, there was a time when many sought to live among the creatures of the great Okefenokee Swamp. Some of them left the evidences of their tenure in the swamp for others to learn from.

On a sunny, but cool, fall day my wife and I traveled to the Chesser Island homestead to attend an old fashioned cane grinding. The homestead is located on the eastern edge of the great Okefenokee Swamp National Wildlife Refuge of southern Georgia near the Florida state line. The homestead is an original homestead dating from 1927 when it was built by Tom and Iva Chesser. Tom was one of the sons of W. T. Chesser who originally settled the island in the late 1800's with his family.

These were the kinds of people who didn't rely on store bought items to survive. Instead, they learned to take what the swamp would give. They used it to build their lives here with the sounds of bull alligators roaring into the night announcing their territorial challenge to all and the never ceasing chatter of crickets, birds, and croaking bull frogs. Nature's own orchestra.

Chesser Island (Pt 2)

by Swampnut

The Chesser family homestead is of the type once found scattered around the edges of the swamp as well as within its watery environs. In 1936 the Okefenokee Swamp was acquired by the federal government. This led to the creation of the National Wildlife Refuge which now occupies the greater part of the swamp habitat. Following this the remaining descendents of the original settlers had to vacate the swamp. Most of them re-settled within the surrounding farming communities.

Yearly, the park service announces various activities and educational opportunities for families and individuals to take part in and usually one or two are located at the old homestead. Every fall the National Park service employees and volunteers who serve at the Suwannee Canal entrance to the wildlife refuge invite the public to a sugar cane grinding exhibition. The exhibition celebrated what was once a family or community yearly tradition in many rural parts of the Deep South

A visit to the homestead and a quiet walk along the trails through the sweet gum, pine, and oak trees can be a peaceful and interesting experience. From the blooming wildflowers, to the various colored mushrooms and lichen spotted tree trunks nature sings out the beauty of the swamps ecosystem. With a careful eye and a little luck one may spot the illusive whitetail deer or, possibly a sunning alligator or turtle in the swampy nearby waters. A visit to the great swamp is well worth the effort and can lead to a greater appreciation of the beauty of natural wonder.

Bubbles in the Okefenokee Swamp

By Swampnut

No, it's not "Bubblews" in case you miss-read the title... though it could be. Nope, it's "bubbles". Historically there have been 3 different types which I am aware of which have existed in the swamp.

First, there are the tell –tell bubbles which escape from the bottom and mark the passage of things like alligators, turtles, and maybe otters as they pass by or below you. I have often had alligators submerge ahead of my canoe and then double back to pass below me in an attempt to get away from me in a narrow channel of water. It isn't that I was pursuing them. It's just that they thought I was. I was simply going forward along a trail towards a place where I would camp or fish.

The second is closely related to the first. Those bubbles which the critters stirred up are actually bubbles of methane gas which, before it was disturbed, rested down below trapped below the decaying vegetation on the bottom. The bottom of the Okefenokee is coated in dead plant material which has been decaying for years. A by-product of this is methane gas. The pressure builds down below and if it isn't prematurely released by a passing critter, the pressure will build to a point and push the decayed material to the surface where it'll float. Eventually plants begin to grow on it.

The third type of bubbles is the kind I heard once or twice as a child. One evening, my dad and I were standing on a remote road near the swamp's edge listening to hounds chase a fox or something. I became aware of a bubbling sound coming out of the area of a cypress pond behind us about 70-100 yards away. When my dad saw me begin to turn around towards the sound he said with a smile,"Son, don't you turn around and look back there. Just ignore that sound." After a few minutes we got in our pickup and left that place to follow the dogs.

After we were on our way, dad explained that he didn't know if the moonshine makers were at their still or not, but he didn't want them to see us look in the direction of the bubbling sound if they were. We talked a little about it, but we didn't go back to that area for several weeks. Not sure if any of those types still hang out around the swamp these days.

Attack of the Raccoons

By Swampnut

Like that title? Well, it was not exactly an attack…more like a raid.

You see, we were canoeing through the Okefenokee Swamp from the east side entrance near Folkston, Georgia, headed for the southwest exit at Stephen Foster State Park.

I had my little brother with me then and a group of boys and men from a church. We were about 15 miles in and had stopped for the night near the end of the Suwannee canal run. We made camp, cooked supper and had plans to sleep peacefully through the night after the many hours of paddling. I knew we might be visited during the night by raccoons or some other critter, so I instructed the group to hang the garbage bag from a high tree limb, which they did. In fact it was hanging slightly out over the edge of the water in which there were alligators going to and fro on their alligator business.

About an hour after sundown, with darkness in full mode, the raccoons began their attack! Padding almost with ghostly silence they suddenly were everywhere! They first made for the canoes and found our full size ice chest in one of them. With almost no effort, they pulled the lid off which landed with a loud clatter in the bottom of the canoe. This loud, unexpectedly loud and echoing, noise seemed to call the alligators to zero in on the raiding raccoons. It also startled the raccoons themselves.

Our guys shot out of their tents to save the food in the ice chest! The raccoons scattered, the alligators whipped to and fro in the water's edge looking for a careless meal...animal or human would probably have been fine with them. The boys quickly secured the ice chest's top with a menagerie of ropes and crisscrossed paddles and whatever other gear they could find. They also canoed out and retrieved a floating vest which one of the raccoons had knocked into the water. This vest had attracted the attention of an alligator so a paddle was used to whack him in the snout and retrieve the vest.

Now, the second wave of the attack was launched! The crafty critters climbed up into the large tree and out on the limb from which our trash was suspended. At that point one of them dove down onto the hanging bag and crashed it to the ground! The trash was everywhere and the buffet was open!

Our guys grabbed paddles and shoes to throw and launched a counter attack to try and save the mess from being carried off into the swamp. After a momentary standoff, the raccoons retreated. The trash was gathered and someone allowed it to be put into their tent for the night. Everyone settled down and lay awake for a while inside their tents recounting their individual acts of bravery to their tent mates (in case they had missed it during the fracas). It was a while before they could sleep after so much excitement.

The next day saw us exit the swamp after a rather difficult push through some very grown over spots along the trails we followed out. We had no further issues with wildlife and the boys (and the men) loved the trip!

For weeks afterwards, boys recounted this night's adventure to anyone at church or school who would listen. I am sure the size and ferocity of the raccoons grew as the stories were told and retold.

Should We Follow Every Trail?

Sometimes, when a man is thinking and dwelling on things in his life which are or have been unsettling to him, his mind wanders down trails of thought which they might not normally follow. These are those times which test what a man says he deeply believes in. His faith in his God, his family, himself. It is in these wanderings that a man will round a curve of a particular trail of thought and be presented with a dilemma of his own making. Many a wanderer of nature's swampy Okefenokee trails will understand this.

A man has entered an area, which for some reason or another; he is not supposed to be in. Temptation has led him this far. He has already failed his first test, yet doesn't know it. " What's around the next bend of the trail?" echoes through his thoughts, dancing here and there like a temptress wearing a flowing silk garment. The picture is not quite clear in his mind but there it is, dancing around the edges leading him to take just one more stroke of the paddle to push his canoe a little deeper into the unknown. That's when the second time of testing is met. As if he had glided around a tall-grass lined curve and suddenly came face to face with a swimming black bear, the thought crashes in, "Do I stay and see what happens next or back paddle to safer waters?".

Many a married man has rounded that curve and suddenly awakened to the danger luring them towards things a married man should not consider. And just as quickly, their faith in their marriage or their family or something else spurs them to action and the imaginary waters are splashed and scattered wildly as he back paddles quickly away from the seductive temptress.

Others have not been so lucky as to have such deeply embedded beliefs or faith. They are still looking for something on which to nail their faith, their belief system. Maybe they were injured deeply by a long lost parent or love. Maybe the corruptions of this world have caused them deep pain and therein damaged whatever faith they proclaimed to have held at an earlier time of life. For them the temptress is a challenger to be pursued and in the pursuing, maybe they hope to find a landing place of faith. A place where they can believe again in someone or something. Where they can find a belief that is real enough to give them courage in times of hurt or danger.

So they paddle forward gliding down the trails of thought, barely hindered, if hindered at all, with thoughts of disappointing anyone. They look for the next bit of excitement, of challenge to overcome, of something to make life worth living again. These men never have a thought for the trail they wander down and why they should not be there. They never look behind them at the damage they are doing with each stroke of their paddled thoughts. As calluses build up on the hands of a man who paddles the long trail from Kingfisher Landing to Billy's Island, so this type of passage builds calluses in the minds of men. They feel less and less of guilt or shame, if they ever felt it at all.

For these men, the temptress is never truly caught. She's here, she's there. They wander onward always looking, seeking, searching. This temptress is like the low wisps of fog on an early morning lily pad decorated prairie of swamp grasses. He can, he thinks, see it clearly and if one wants to do so, paddle over to it and touch it. Yet, when he gets there... it has moved. Yet, it seems so real! Off "over there" he sees it again, this time with red-winged blackbirds dipping in and out of it and sitting just above its wavy top on tips of strong tall grasses.

So, off he goes, to follow it and hopefully touch this thing of ghostly beauty. And the wandering continues.

****

There are many thought trails in life which men can freely wander down without doing any serious damage to themselves or those people and things they hold dear. And there are others, old as time itself, which are there tempting us to look around the next bend, to follow, to explore their possibilities. Those trails are best left alone, those temptations best not accepted. There is an old story told of Obediah Barber, that great man of the swamp. Seems there was an old lady who lived alone on a little island in the swamp. She was known to be a witch, but Obediah wasn't afraid of her and would talk to her from time to time. One day on one of her visits to Obediah's home, she told him that when she died she would come back and visit him. After some time, she passed away. A few days later Obediah was riding his horse from Jim Hendrix's house to his home after dark when suddenly, there stood the old woman in the middle of the trail!

The story goes that Obediah simply walked his horse a little off to the side and passed her while tipping his hat and saying "Good evening." She never spoke and he didn't stop. When he looked back, she was gone.* Many of us would do well to heed his example and not linger when tempted by circumstances that we shouldn't be dealing with.

In the book of Proverbs in the Bible, that ancient book of wisdom, we see this, "A righteous man who walks in his integrity – How blessed are his sons after him." (Proverbs 20:7) So, even if we say we will throw caution to the wind and head off in a direction we shouldn't go, just remember; your actions will definitely affect others you love.

Bottom line: *Some trails in life are best left unfollowed.*

_____

* Obediah story is from <u>Tips from Tau: the Okefenokee Swamp an Educational Opportunity</u> compiled, edited, and illustrated by members of Tau Chapter, Psi State Delta Kappa Gamma. Printed by Hebardville Printing Co., Waycross, Ga. (Date unknown).

A Bear, a Deer, and some Unfortunate Bushes

By Swampnut

During my years of growing up near the Okefenokee there was a period of time when many people from my town would deer hunt along the edges of the great swamp. At about the time I was around 14 or 15 years of age, this story took place.

One day my dad and I had been riding the small dirt roads in a region along the edge of the swamp looking for deer tracks across the road. I had two pretty little black and tan beagles and if we could find fresh sign, we hoped to see if they would chase the deer. If they would and if they would bay along the way, we would try to get ahead of him. A good shot would allow us to have venison in the freezer for a while. These days I don't hunt with hounds but back then in the 1960's it was a very common thing.

We had not found any sign so finally, I asked my dad to allow me to enter the woods and follow a firebreak around to the end of a nearby dead end road. The walk would have been about a mile or so. I would be following the edge of a "branch", an area of thick brush and trees with a small creek running through it.

I entered the woods following my beagles. They ran all around sniffing here and there and enjoying themselves. My dad left and drove on over to the end of the nearby road to wait for me. About a hundred yards into the woods, suddenly my little playful beagles were all business! They were growling and with hair standing on end they came back to stay near me! Within a few feet I found fresh sign of where an animal had pooped….and a few feet further a very clear track in the mud of the firebreak…a bear track! Now my hair was standing on end and I was almost breathless. My mouth was cottony dry. I was simply scared!

After looking all around and not seeing or hearing anything over the sound of my pounding heart and my growling beagles, we pushed on towards where I would meet my dad. After walking about a half mile or more, I was relaxed and so were the dogs. Nothing was around it seemed. I figured we were not going to see a deer so I changed out my buckshot for birdshot. I had spotted a squirrel nest and thought I might find a squirrel to shoot. Within a couple of minutes everything changed!

My dogs suddenly started barking! I looked up and there he was! A huge buck leaping over palmetto bushes in leisurely fashion as if he was in a Disney movie! He had a huge set of antlers! And then he heard the dogs and started running swiftly through the palmettos and ceased his leaping. I was frantically reloading my gun with buckshot. My dogs were yelping and running back and forth as if they were saying, "Hurry up, hurry up!"

I rushed on a short distance to the end of the road where my dad had been waiting. He had jumped into his pickup and left to rush down to the junction to see if he might be able to intercept the big deer. I was there now on the road with my excited beagles milling about... and as I looked out into the woods, my eyes focused on what I thought was the big deer simply standing there looking at me. It didn't quite look right but I was so excited, I thought it was him and I shot... and watched a brownish clump of palmetto bushes wave back at me as the buckshot ripped through the bushes.

A bit later my dad came driving back up and when I told him what I had done; he lectured me on how that was not a good thing to do. He had told me many times before that I should never shoot unless I was sure of what I was shooting at and he reinforced that lesson once again.

Since that day, I have never fired at, through or into bushes. Safety comes first.

What happened to the deer and bear? Never saw them!

Ole' Ridge Back

In a land of moss and water,

Slowly floats a ridged-backed fellow.

Seeming slow as coming Christmas

He'll explode with stunning swiftness.

Which explains the sudden loss,

Of little Jimmy's golden cross.

The one he wore around his neck,

Given him by Sally Beck.

One hot day while on the water,

With his fishing gear in order,

Little Jimmy bent to sip,

A drink to cool his burning lip.

With lily pads erupting and water flying high,

Ole' Ridge-Back snapped his jaws…

On a swinging golden bar!

By Clint Bowman, 1996

Conclusion:

I hope you have enjoyed at least some parts of this little book. The Okefenokee is a great place to fish and camp. Those who enjoy bird watching and photography will love it. If you have never had the pleasure of visiting the swamp, the links below will help you as you plan your first trip.

The Okefenokee Heritage Center located in Waycross, Georgia, is also a good place to enjoy some of the area's history and art created by Okefenokee inspired artists. Their link is below also.

Thanks for reading,

Clint "Swampnut" Bowman

https://www.facebook.com/pages/Okefenokee-Heritage-Center/155266257839657

http://gastateparks.org/StephenCFoster

http://www.okefenokee.com/info/info/

http://www.okeswamp.com/

These books may also be helpful:

The Okefenokee Swamp by Franklin Russell (and the editors of Time Life books)

Okefenokee Swamp: Wild and Natural by Wayne Morgan and Don Berryhill

Trembling Earth: A Cultural History of the Okefenokee Swamp by Megan Kate Nelson

There are many more books which you can find online about the Okefenokee. The gift shops at the various park entrances also usually have a few in stock.